Stark County District Library
www.StarkLibrary.org
330.452.0665

MAY -- 2019

S0-EIL-121

COELOPHYSIS

by Arnold Ringstad

Cody Koala

An Imprint of Pop!

popbooksonline.com

abdobooks.com

Published by Pop!, a division of ABDO, PO Box 398166, Minneapolis, Minnesota 55439. Copyright © 2019 by POP, LLC. International copyrights reserved in all countries. No part of this book may be reproduced in any form without written permission from the publisher. Pop!™ is a trademark and logo of POP, LLC.

Printed in the United States of America, North Mankato, Minnesota

082018
012019

THIS BOOK CONTAINS
RECYCLED MATERIALS

Cover Photo: iStockphoto

Interior Photos: iStockphoto, 1, 9, 11; Roger Hall/Science Source, 5; Arterra Picture Library/Alamy, 6; Mark Hallett Paleoart/Science Source, 12; Shutterstock Images, 15; Christian Jegou/Publiphoto/Science Source, 17; Millard H. Sharp/Science Source, 19 (top); Francois Gohier/Science Source, 19 (bottom left), 19 (bottom right); De Agostini Picture Library/Science Source, 20

Editor: Meg Gaertner
Series Designer: Laura Mitchell

Library of Congress Control Number: 2018949755

Publisher's Cataloging-in-Publication Data

Names: Ringstad, Arnold, author.
Title: Coelophysis / by Arnold Ringstad.
Description: Minneapolis, Minnesota : Pop!, 2019 | Series: Dinosaurs | Includes online resources and index.
Identifiers: ISBN 9781532161797 (lib. bdg.) | ISBN 9781641855501 (pbk.) | ISBN 9781532162855 (ebook)
Subjects: LCSH: Coelophysis--Juvenile literature. | Dinosaurs--Juvenile literature. | Extinct animals--Juvenile literature.
Classification: DDC 567.912--dc23

Hello! My name is

Cody Koala

Pop open this book and you'll find QR codes like this one, loaded with information, so you can learn even more!

Scan this code* and others like it while you read, or visit the website below to make this book pop.

popbooksonline.com/coelophysis

*Scanning QR codes requires a web-enabled smart device with a QR code reader app and a camera.

Table of Contents

Chapter 1

A Speedy Predator

Coelophysis was a meat-eating dinosaur. It was about 10 feet long. This is a little shorter than mid-size cars. It weighed as much as a large dog.

Watch a video here!

This **predator** had sharp teeth and claws. It used its front claws to grab bugs and small animals.

The name Coelophysis is pronounced "seel-OH-fie-sis."

Coelophysis ran on two strong legs. It moved quickly. Its long tail helped it move.

Coelophysis had large eyes. This helped it hunt small **prey.**

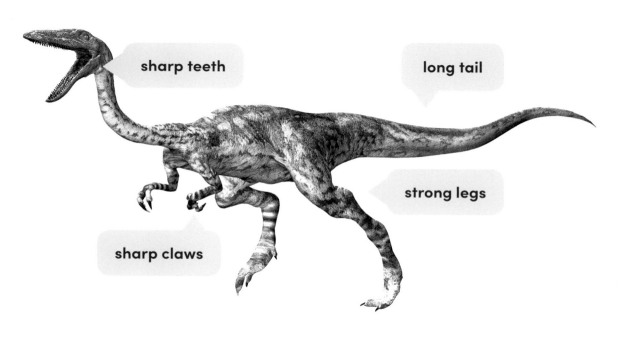

Chapter 2

Hollow Bones

The name Coelophysis means "hollow form." This dinosaur had hollow bones. They had an empty space inside.

Learn more here!

The hollow bones kept Coelophysis's weight low. Being light helped it move fast and catch prey.

Birds have hollow bones too. This makes them light enough to fly. Dinosaurs **evolved** into the birds we see today.

Living in the Triassic

Coelophysis was one of the first dinosaurs. It lived about 220 million years ago. This was in the **Triassic Period**. Early dinosaurs appeared during this time.

Coelophysis

Complete an activity here!

Digging Up Bones

Scientists dug up the first
Coelophysis bones in 1881.
In 1947, scientists found
hundreds of skeletons
together in New Mexico.

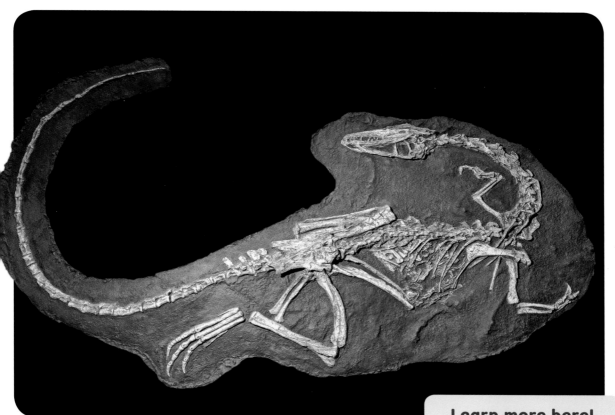

Learn more here!

Many skeletons were found together. Scientists think this may show how the dinosaur lived. It may have lived or hunted in **packs**.

Coelophysis is the official state **fossil** of New Mexico.

Making Connections

Text-to-Self

Scientists dig up fossils to learn more about how dinosaurs lived. Would you ever want to study fossils? Why or why not?

Text-to-Text

Have you read any other books about dinosaurs? What did you learn?

Text-to-World

Scientists think Coelophysis may have hunted in packs. Have you seen any animals today that hunt in groups like this?

Glossary

evolved – changed over millions of years.

fossil – the remains of a plant or an animal from a long time ago.

pack – a group of animals that live and hunt together.

predator – an animal that hunts other animals.

prey – an animal that is hunted by other animals.

Triassic Period – a period that lasted from about 250 million years ago to about 200 million years ago.

Index

Online Resources

popbooksonline.com

Thanks for reading this Cody Koala book!

Scan this code* and others like it in this book, or visit the website below to make this book pop!

popbooksonline.com/coelophysis

*Scanning QR codes requires a web-enabled smart device with a QR code reader app and a camera.

9 781532 161797